UNDERSTANDING JONAH

A Commentary on the Book of Jonah using Ancient Bible Study Methods – UPDATED

Michael H. Koplitz

CONTENTS

ACKNOWLEDGMENTS

This work could not have been accomplished without Dr. Anne Davis, who taught me Ancient (Hebraic) Bible study methods, and my two study partners, Rev. Dr. Robert Cook and Pastor Sandra Koplitz. We know the journey has just started and will last a lifetime. The discovery of the depths of God's Word is waiting for us to find.

Introduction

While I was attending Seminary earning my M. Div. degree, I questioned what the instructors and reference books, which were required, were saying about the Scriptures. One idea being offered then was that the Bible was full of errors and not factual. I found that attitude disturbing for Seminary instructors to be teaching. After all, the Seminary experience is to train pastors to go out into God's world and preach the Bible. How can you preach the Bible if you believe what these instructors are teaching? The methods that were being taught to examine the Bible just seemed inaccurate to me.

After graduating from Seminary, I spent a lot of time reading different views about the

Bible. I eventually reached the Zohar. Kabbalists consider this collection of midrash as the secret work of the Torah. In addition, I read quite a bit about Messianic Judaism. Their view of the Bible differs greatly from the Seminary view.

I decided that the biblical interpretation that was being taught in Seminary, was not the biblical interpretation the people heard when Jesus Christ (whose Hebraic name is Yeshua) preached. I went on a quest to learn what the people of Yeshua's day heard, and what they thought when the Scriptures were read. This quest led me to Dr. Anne Davis and The Bible Learning University. Dr. Davis was in search of the same thing I was searching for. She had made many discoveries that helped me in my quest. I earned the Ph.D. degree from The Bible Learning University in Hebraic Studies in Christianity concentrating on ancient Bible Studies methods.

Finally, I found someone who believed that the church has placed almost 1900 years of their theological ideas about the Scriptures, which differed from the original Hebraic thoughts, and in many places, possibly misinterpreted its original meaning. What is also important to hear is that the basic tenants of Yeshua as God's Messiah, my LORD and Savior are in the Bible. My faith in Yeshua is stronger now that I have learned from Dr. Davis how to study the Scriptures in the same manner that the people did in Yeshua's day.

I have included some articles that describe the differences between Greek learning methods and Hebraic learning methods. Please do not skip by them as irrelevant, unless you are familiar with the ancient Bible student method, because if you do, then the analysis and commentary that follows may become difficult to understand.

Our God is vast and infinite and so is His Word. May God bless you in your discovery of what God's Word is about.

In that vein of thought, we can consider the book of Jonah in light of Yeshua the Messiah. My study partner, Sandy, asked me if there is anything important to the name Jonah. As I considered this question I thought about the meaning of the word Jonah. This Hebrew word means "peace." A dove is first encountered in the Noah story. When the rain had stopped and the water started to recede, Noah sent a dove out to look for dry land. When the dove returned with an olive branch, Noah knew that the world had been transformed by God. The world restarted in peace and love.

When Yeshua was baptized in the Jordan River by John a dove came down from Heaven. The belief is that the dove is symbolic of the Holy Spirit. The love and grace of God descended upon the Earth in a "new form." Through the Holy Spirit the disciples of Yeshua brought God's love to a violent world. Yeshua preached that the Kingdom of God could be established on the Earth. A key component of the Kingdom of God is peace.

Can the Jonah story be viewed as a story

about peace? Making peace with your enemies is not the main theme of the story but it certainly can be a tributary of the main theme. Historically it is known that the Assyrian Empire (Ninevites) was an enemy to many nations. The Northern Kingdom (Israel) and the Southern Kingdom (Judah) would have viewed Assyria as an enemy.

So, God sent a Hebrew prophet to Nineveh to bring a message to the people about repentance. Could another purpose of Jonah's mission to Nineveh be as a peace maker? Why would a representative who viewed Nineveh as an enemy come to the city to warn it that the LORD was going to destroy them if they did not repent from their evil ways? The Middle Eastern nations and tribe who were conquered by the Assyrians would have been joyful if the LORD had destroyed the Empire before it had a chance to destroy them. Jonah's attempt to save Nineveh could be viewed as a message of peace. Could the Assyrians have viewed the Hebrews as a friend instead of an enemy?

You are probably thinking, the Assyrians destroyed the Northern Kingdom, so peace did not happen. However, the prophecy of the book of Jonah never happened. The Ninevites did not repent of their evil ways. Their Empire conquered the nations and tribes in the Middle East and they did some of the worst things you can do to a fellow human.

Since the prophecy did not come true, neither did the peace that was hoped. If the people of Nineveh would have repented and changed their way then the Hebrew people would have become their friends.

For us today, in the light of Yeshua, this story can tell us that we should make an effort to become friends with our enemies. Yeshua tells us to love our enemies in Matthew 5:44. The first step to loving an enemy is to make peace with them. Offering a gesture of some kind, to soft the heart of the enemy, may indeed work. Telling Nineveh about God's wrath and how to avoid it was the gesture to opening the door to peace. Loving our enemy might start by offering a gesture of peace. If we were all peacemakers, war would be eliminated from the world.

Jonah was the son of Amittai who lived during the reign of Amaziah, king of Judah and Jeroboam II, king of Israel. The time frame was the first half of the eighth century B.C.E. (2 Kings 14:23-25). Jonah believed that the God of Israel and Judah was not the God of the Gentile nations who surrounded the Promised Land.

During Jonah's lifetime the Assyrian Empire grew to the west and south of the River Euphrates. Israel and Judah could not escape from the power of the Assyrian Empire and eventually fell victim. It was through Jonah's prophecy that the Hebrews realized that their God was also the God of the Gentiles. They also believed that God had empowered the Assyrians to punish them for their misdeeds and their pagan worship practices.

Jonah's vision from God was to take a message to the Assyrians about their deeds. Jonah resisted, probably because it was hard for him to accept that the God of the Hebrews would pardon a potential enemy. Jonah discovered that the LORD existed everywhere because even though he tried to run away the LORD found him.

Jonah submitted to the LORD and delivered the message. Jonah became angry when he saw that the Gentiles accepted the LORD's message and repented while prophets were in Israel and Judah who offered the same message were being ignored.

The Main Difference between the Greek Method and the Hebraic Method of Teaching

Once you are aware of the two teaching styles, you will determine if you are in a class or reading a book, whether the analysis and/or teaching method is in a Greek or Hebraic method. In the Greek method, the instructor is right because of advanced knowledge. In the college situation, it is because the professor has his/her Ph.D. in some areas of study, so one assumes that he or she knows everything about the topic. For example, Rodney Dangerfield played the role of a middle-aged man going to college. His English midterm was to write about Kurt Vonnegut Jr. Since he didn't understand any of Vonnegut's books, he hired Vonnegut himself to the write the midterm. When it was returned to him, the English Professor told Dangerfield that whoever wrote the paper knew nothing about Vonnegut. This is an example of the Greek method of teaching. Did the Ph.D. English professor think that she knew more about Vonnegut's writings than Vonnegut did?[1]

In the Greek teaching method, the professor or the instructor claims to be the authority. If you are attending a Bible study class and the class leader says, "I will teach you the only way to understand this biblical book," you may want to consider the implications. This method is common since most Seminaries and Bible colleges teach a Greek method of learning, which is the same method the

---

[1] *Back to School*. Performed by Rodney Dangerfield. Hollywood: CA: Paper Clip Productions, 1986. DVD.

church has been utilizing for centuries.

Hebraic teaching methods are different. The teacher wants the students to challenge what they hear. It is through questioning that a student can learn. In addition, the teacher wants his/her students to excel to a point where the student becomes the teacher.

It is said that if two rabbis come together to discuss a passage of Scripture, the result will be at least ten different opinions. All points of view are acceptable as long as the points can be supported by biblical evidence. It is permissible and encourages students to have multiple opinions. There is a depth to God's Word, and God wants us to find all His messages that are placed in the Scriptures.

Seeking out the meaning of the Scriptures beyond the literal meaning is essential to fully understanding God's Word.[2] The Greek method of learning the Scriptures has prevailed over the centuries. One problem is that only the literal interpretation of Scripture was often viewed as valid, as prompted by Martin Luther's "sola literalis" meaning that only the literal interpretation of Scripture was valid. The Fundamentalist movements of today are generally based on the literal interpretation of the Scripture. Therefore, they do not believe that God placed any deeper, hidden, or secret meanings in the Word.

The students of the Scriptures who learn through Hebraic training and understanding have drawn a different conclusion. The Hebrew language itself leads to different

---

[2] Davis, Anne Kimball. *The Synoptic Gospels*. MP3. Albuquerque: NM: BibleInteract, 2012.

possible interpretations because of the construction of the language. The Hebraic method of Bible study opens avenues of thought about God's revelations in the Scripture that may have never been considered. A question may be raised about the Scripture being studied for which there may not be an immediate answer. If so, it becomes the responsibility of the learners to uncover the meaning. Also, remember that multiple opinions about the meaning of Scripture are also acceptable if they can be supported by Scripture.

Methodology

The method employed is to use First Century Scripture study methods integrated with the customs and culture of Yeshua's day to examine the Hebrew and Christian Scriptures, thus gathering a deeper understanding by learning the Scriptures in the way the people of Yeshua's day did.

In typical Rabbinic tradition, I had two study partners. Each one served a different function by looking at the research as I put it together. Rev. Dr. Robert Cook, D. Min., an ordained Elder in the United Methodist Church, has been a study partner in different areas of theology and church leadership. He became interested in Hebraic studies when I started sharing Zohar and Midrash with him. He also completed the entire Disciple program as a student and teacher. My second study partner is my wife, Sandra Koplitz, MS. Sandy and I took the instruction class on teaching the Disciple Bible study program and she takes part in the Zohar study group. Sandy is a licensed local pastor in the United Methodist Church.

The Process of Discovery

I have titled the method of analyzing a passage of Scripture in a Hebraic manner the "Process of Discovery." The author, bringing together the various areas of linguistic and cultural understanding, developed this method. There are several sections to the process, and not all the sections apply to every passage of Scripture. The overall result of developing this process is to give the reader a framework into the ideas being presented.

The "Process of Discovery" starts with a Scripture passage. If the passage takes a poetic form, it is identified. Possible poetic techniques include parallelism, chiastic structures, and repetition. Formatting the passage in its poetic form allows the reader to visualize what the first century CE listener was hearing. Any parallelism is shown with colored text and the chiasms are labeled by their corresponding sections, for example: A, B, C, B', A'. Not all passages of the Scriptures have a poetic form.

The next step is to "question the narrative," which is accomplished by assuming the reader knows nothing about the passage. Therefore, the questions go from the simple to the complex. The next task is to identify any linguistic patterns. Linguistic patterns include, but are not limited to: irony, simile, metaphor, symbolism, idioms, hyperbole, figurative language, personification, and allegory.

We identify any translation inconsistencies between the English NASB version and either the Hebrew or Greek versions. Sometimes a Hebrew or Greek word can be translated in more than one way. Inconsistencies also can be created by the translation committee, which may have used traditional language instead of the actual translation. The Preface or Introduction to the Bible contains the decision of the translation committee. Perhaps the translation committee intentionally added some inconsistencies to convey a deeper meaning, so we need to examine the inconsistencies.

Scholars identify echoes of the Hebrew Scriptures in the Christian Scripture. This occurs when a passage from the Hebrew

Scripture is used in the Christian Scripture or when a Mitzvah is directly discussed in the Christian Scriptures.[3] In addition, echoes can be found when Torah (Genesis through Deuteronomy) passages are used in other Hebrew Bible books. Besides echoes, cross-references are listed. A cross reference is a reference to another verse in the Scripture which can assist the reader to understand the verse that is being read.

The names of people mentioned in the passage are listed. Many of the Hebrew names have meaning and may be associated with places or actions. Jewish parents used to name their children based on what they felt God had in store for their child. An example of this is Abraham, whose original name was Abram,

---

[3] Mitzvot are the 613 commandments found in the Torah that please God. There are positive and negative commandments. The list was first development by Maimonides. The full list can be found at: ttp://www.jewfaq.org/613.htm.

and was changed to mean eternal father (in this case God changed Abram's name to Abraham, showing a function he was to perform). When the Hebrew Bible gives names, many of the occurrences will show something special to the reader/listener. The same importance can hold true for the names of places. The time to travel between places can supply insight to the event.

Keywords are identified in a verse when they are important to an understanding of that passage. There are no rules for selecting the keywords. Searching for other occurrences of the keywords in Scripture in a concordance is necessary to understand how the word was being used; this must be done in either Hebrew or Greek, not in English. A classic Hebraic approach is to find the usage of a word in the Scripture by finding other verses that contain the word. The usage of a word, in its original language, is discovered by searching for the Scripture in the word's language. The verses that contain the word being researched are identified and a pattern for the usage of the word is discerned. Each verse is examined to see what the usage of the word is which, may reveal a pattern for the word's usage. For Hebrew words, the first usage of the word in the Scripture, especially if used in the Torah, is important. For the Greek words, the Christian Scriptures are used to determining the word usage in the Scripture. Sometimes finding the equivalent Greek word in the Septuagint and then analyzing its usage in Hebrew can be very helpful.

The Rules of Hillel for Bible understanding can be used when applicable. Hillel was a

Torah scholar who lived shortly before Yeshua's day. Hillel developed several rules for Torah students to interpret the Scriptures which are referred to as halachic midrash. These rules are helpful in the analysis of the Scripture in several cases.

After the linguistic analysis is complete, an examination of the cultural implications will be examined. The culture is important because it is not specifically referenced in the biblical narratives as indicated earlier.

From linguistic analysis and the cultural understanding, it is possible to get a deeper meaning of the Scripture beyond the literal meaning of the plaintext. That is what the listeners of Yeshua's time were doing. They put linguistics and the culture together without even having to contemplate it. They simply did it.

This will lead to a conclusion or a set of conclusions about what the passage is talking about. Most of the time, the Hebraic analysis leads to the desire for a deeper analysis to fully understand what Yeshua was talking about or what was happening to Him. Whatever the result, a new deeper understanding of the Scripture will be obtained.

The components of the Process of Discovery are:

Linguistics Section

Linguistic Structure of the Scripture

Discussion

Questioning the Passage

(Answers to these questions are offered for discussion and you may have different answers. Remember, answers must be defendable from Scripture. In addition, you may have additional questions about the passage that is not covered. This applies to this section and to the Questioning the Passage in the Cultural section.)

Main/Center Point

Verse Comparison of citations or proof text

Idioms

Metaphors

Symbols

Translation inconsistencies

People's names

Name of places

Word Study

Topics

Scripture cross references

Echoes

Rules of Hillel

Culture Section

Discussion

Questioning the passage culturally

Culture and Linguistics Section

Discussion

Only the sections pertinent to each chapter of Jonah are included.

Jonah Chapter One

New American Standard 1995	Hebrew	Septuagint
¹ The word of the LORD came to Jonah the son of Amittai saying, ² "Arise, go to Nineveh the great city and cry against it, for their	¹וַֽיְהִי֙ דְּבַר־יְהוָ֔ה אֶל־יוֹנָ֥ה בֶן־אֲמִתַּ֖י לֵאמֹֽר: ²ק֠וּם לֵ֧ךְ אֶל־נִֽינְוֵ֛ה הָעִ֥יר הַגְּדוֹלָ֖ה וּקְרָ֣א עָלֶ֑יהָ כִּֽי־עָלְתָ֥ה רָעָתָ֖ם לְפָנָֽי: ³וַיָּ֣קָם יוֹנָ֗ה	¹ Now the word of the LORD came to Jonas the son of Amathi, saying, ² Rise, and go to Nineve, the great city, and preach

New American Standard 1995	Hebrew	Septuagint
wickedness has come up before Me." ³ But Jonah rose up to flee to Tarshish from the presence of the LORD. So he went down to Joppa, found a ship which was going to	לִבְרֹחַ תַּרְשִׁישָׁה מִלִּפְנֵי יְהוָה וַיֵּרֶד יָפוֹ וַיִּמְצָא אָנִיָּה ׀ בָּאָה תַרְשִׁישׁ וַיִּתֵּן שְׂכָרָהּ וַיֵּרֶד בָּהּ לָבוֹא עִמָּהֶם תַּרְשִׁישָׁה מִלִּפְנֵי יְהוָה׃ ⁴וַיהוָה הֵטִיל רוּחַ־גְּדוֹלָה	in it; for the cry of its wickedness is come up to me. ³ But Jonas rose up to flee to Tharsis from the presence of the LORD. And he went down to Joppa, and

New American Standard 1995	Hebrew	Septuagint
Tarshish, paid the fare and went down into it to go with them to Tarshish from the presence of the LORD. 4 The LORD hurled a great wind on the sea and there was a great storm on the	אֱל־הַיָּם וַיְהִי סַעַר־גָּדוֹל בַּיָּם וְהָאֳנִיָּה חִשְּׁבָה לְהִשָּׁבֵר׃ 5 וַיִּירְאוּ הַמַּלָּחִים וַיִּזְעֲקוּ אִישׁ אֶל־אֱלֹהָיו וַיָּטִלוּ אֶת־הַכֵּלִים אֲשֶׁר בָּאֳנִיָּה אֶל־הַיָּם	found a ship going to Tharsis: and he paid his fare, and went up into it, to sail with them to Tharsis from the presence of the LORD. 4 And the LORD raised up a

New American Standard 1995	Hebrew	Septuagint
sea so that the ship was about to break up. 5 Then the sailors became afraid and every man cried to his god, and they threw the cargo which was in the ship into the sea to	לְהָקֵל מֵעֲלֵיהֶם וְיוֹנָה יָרַד אֶל־יַרְכְּתֵי הַסְּפִינָה וַיִּשְׁכַּב וַיֵּרָדַם: 6 וַיִּקְרַב אֵלָיו רַב הַחֹבֵל וַיֹּאמֶר לוֹ מַה־לְּךָ נִרְדָּם קוּם קְרָא אֶל־אֱלֹהֶיךָ אוּלַי	wind on the sea; and there was a great storm on the sea, and the ship was in danger of being broken. 5 And the sailors were alarmed, and cried every one to his

New American Standard 1995	Hebrew	Septuagint
lighten *it* for them. But Jonah had gone below into the hold of the ship, lain down and fallen sound asleep. [6] So the captain approached him and said, "How is it that you are	יִתְעַשֵּׁת הָאֱלֹהִים לָנוּ וְלֹא נֹאבֵד: [7] וַיֹּאמְרוּ אִישׁ אֶל־רֵעֵהוּ לְכוּ וְנַפִּילָה גוֹרָלוֹת וְנֵדְעָה בְּשֶׁלְּמִי הָרָעָה הַזֹּאת לָנוּ וַיַּפִּלוּ גּוֹרָלוֹת וַיִּפֹּל הַגּוֹרָל	god, and cast out the wares that were in the ship into the sea, that it might be lightened of them. But Jonas was gone down into the hold of the ship, and was asleep, and

New American Standard 1995	Hebrew	Septuagint
sleeping? Get up, call on your god. Perhaps *your* god will be concerned about us so that we will not perish." ⁷ Each man said to his mate, "Come, let us cast lots so we may learn on	עַל־יוֹנָה׃ ⁸וַיֹּאמְרוּ אֵלָיו הַגִּידָה־נָּא לָנוּ בַּאֲשֶׁר לְמִי־הָרָעָה הַזֹּאת לָנוּ מַה־מְּלַאכְתְּךָ וּמֵאַיִן תָּבוֹא מָה אַרְצֶךָ וְאֵי־מִזֶּה עַם אָתָּה׃	snored. ⁶ And the shipmaster came to him, and said to him, Why snorest thou? arise, and call upon thy God, that God may save us, and we perish

New American Standard 1995	Hebrew	Septuagint
whose account this calamity *has struck* us." So they cast lots and the lot fell on Jonah. 8 Then they said to him, "Tell us, now! On whose account *has* this calamity *struck* us? What is your	9 וַיֹּ֥אמֶר אֲלֵיהֶ֖ם עִבְרִ֣י אָנֹ֑כִי וְאֶת־יְהֹוָ֞ה אֱלֹהֵ֤י הַשָּׁמַ֙יִם֙ אֲנִ֣י יָרֵ֔א אֲשֶׁר־עָשָׂ֥ה אֶת־הַיָּ֖ם וְאֶת־הַיַּבָּשָֽׁה׃ 10 וַיִּֽירְא֤וּ הָֽאֲנָשִׁים֙ יִרְאָ֣ה גְדוֹלָ֔ה וַיֹּאמְר֥וּ	not. 7 And each man said to his neighbour, Come, let us cast lots, and find out for whose sake this mischief is upon us. So they cast lots, and the lot fell upon

New American Standard 1995	Hebrew	Septuagint
occupation? And where do you come from? What is your country? From what people are you?" 9 He said to them, "I am a Hebrew, and I fear the LORD God of heaven who made the	אֵלָיו מַה־זֹּאת עָשִׂיתָ כִּי־יָדְעוּ הָאֲנָשִׁים כִּי־מִלִּפְנֵי יְהוָה הוּא בֹרֵחַ כִּי הִגִּיד לָהֶם: 11 וַיֹּאמְרוּ אֵלָיו מַה־נַּעֲשֶׂה לָּךְ וְיִשְׁתֹּק הַיָּם מֵעָלֵינוּ כִּי הַיָּם	Jonas. 8 And they said to him, Tell us what is thine occupation, and whence comest thou, and of what country and what people art thou? 9 And he said to them,

New American Standard 1995	Hebrew	Septuagint
sea and the dry land." ¹⁰ Then the men became extremely frightened and they said to him, "How could you do this?" For the men knew that he was fleeing from the presence of the	הוֹלֵךְ וְסֹעֵר: ¹² וַיֹּאמֶר אֲלֵיהֶם שָׂאוּנִי וַהֲטִילֻנִי אֶל־הַיָּם וְיִשְׁתֹּק הַיָּם מֵעֲלֵיכֶם כִּי יוֹדֵעַ אָנִי כִּי בְשֶׁלִּי הַסַּעַר הַגָּדוֹל הַזֶּה עֲלֵיכֶם: ¹³ וַיַּחְתְּרוּ	I am a servant of the LORD; and I worship the LORD God of heaven, who made the sea, and the dry *land*. ¹⁰ Then the men feared exceedingly, and said to him, What is

New American Standard 1995	Hebrew	Septuagint
LORD, because he had told them. 11 So they said to him, "What should we do to you that the sea may become calm for us?"-- for the sea was becoming increasingly	הָאֲנָשִׁים לְהָשִׁיב אֶל־הַיַּבָּשָׁה וְלֹא יָכֹלוּ כִּי הַיָּם הוֹלֵךְ וְסֹעֵר עֲלֵיהֶם: 14 וַיִּקְרְאוּ אֶל־יְהוָה וַיֹּאמְרוּ אָנָּה יְהוָה אַל־נָא נֹאבְדָה בְּנֶפֶשׁ הָאִישׁ	this *that* thou hast done? for the men knew that he was fleeing from the face of the LORD, because he had told them. 11 And they said to him, What shall we do to

New American Standard 1995	Hebrew	Septuagint
stormy. [12] He said to them, "Pick me up and throw me into the sea. Then the sea will become calm for you, for I know that on account of me this great storm *has come*	הַזֶּ֥ה וְאַל־תִּתְּ֛ן עָלֵ֖ינוּ דָּ֣ם נָקִ֑יא כִּֽי־אַתָּ֣ה יְהוָ֔ה כַּאֲשֶׁ֥ר חָפַ֖צְתָּ עָשִֽׂיתָ׃ [15] וַיִּשְׂאוּ֙ אֶת־יוֹנָ֔ה וַיְטִלֻ֖הוּ אֶל־הַיָּ֑ם וַיַּעֲמֹ֥ד הַיָּ֖ם מִזַּעְפּֽוֹ׃ [16] וַיִּֽירְא֧וּ	thee, that the sea may be calm to us? for the sea rose, and lifted its wave exceedingly. [12] And Jonas said to them, Take me up, and cast me into the sea, and the sea shall

New American Standard 1995	Hebrew	Septuagint
upon you." 13 However, the men rowed *desperately* to return to land but they could not, for the sea was becoming *even* stormier against them. 14 Then they called on the	הָאֲנָשִׁים יִרְאָ֤ה גְדוֹלָ֖ה אֶת־יְהוָ֑ה וַיִּזְבְּחוּ־זֶ֙בַח֙ לַֽיהוָ֔ה וַיִּדְּר֖וּ נְדָרִֽים:	be calm to you: for I know that for my sake this great tempest is upon you. 13 And the men tried hard to return to the land, and were not able: for the sea rose and

New American Standard 1995	Hebrew	Septuagint
LORD and said, "We earnestly pray, O LORD, do not let us perish on account of this man's life and do not put innocent blood on us; for You, O LORD, have done as You		grew more and more tempestuous against them. [14] And they cried to the LORD, and said, Forbid it, LORD: let us not perish for the sake of this man's life, and bring not

New American Standard 1995	Hebrew	Septuagint
have pleased." 15 So they picked up Jonah, threw him into the sea, and the sea stopped its raging. 16 Then the men feared the LORD greatly, and they offered a		righteous blood upon us: for thou, LORD, hast done as thou wouldest. 15 So they took Jonas, and cast him out into the sea: and the sea ceased from its raging.

New American Standard 1995	Hebrew	Septuagint
sacrifice to the LORD and made vows. 17 And the LORD appointed a great fish to swallow Jonah, and Jonah was in the stomach of the fish three days and three		16 And the men feared the LORD very greatly, and offered a sacrifice to the LORD, and vowed vows.

New American Standard 1995	Hebrew	Septuagint
nights.		

Process of Discovery

Linguistics Section

Linguistic Structure

[Commandment from the LORD][1] The word of the LORD came to Jonah the son of Amittai saying, [2] "Arise, go to Nineveh the great city and cry against it, for their wickedness has come up before Me."

[Rejection of the command] [3] But Jonah rose up to flee to Tarshish from the presence of the LORD. So he went down to Joppa, found a ship which was going to Tarshish, paid the fare and went down into it to go with them to Tarshish from the presence of the LORD.

A [4] The LORD hurled a great wind on the sea and **there was a great storm on the sea** so that the ship was about to break up. [5]

Then the sailors became afraid and every man cried to his god, and they threw the cargo which was in the ship into the sea to lighten *it* for them. But Jonah had gone below into the hold of the ship, lain down and fallen sound asleep.

B [6] So the captain approached him and said, "How is it that you are sleeping? Get up, call on your god. Perhaps *your* god will be concerned about us so that we will not perish." [7] Each man said to his mate, "Come, let us cast lots so we may learn on whose account this calamity *has struck* us." So they cast lots and the lot fell on Jonah. [8] Then they said to him, "Tell us, now! **On whose account *has* this calamity *struck* us?** What is your occupation? And where do you come from? What is your country? From what people are you?"

C [Jonah's words] [9] He said to them, "I am a Hebrew, and I fear the LORD God of heaven who made the sea and the dry land."

> **D [People's words]** [10] Then the men became extremely frightened and they said to him, "How could you do this?"

>> **E** For the men knew that he was fleeing from the presence of the LORD, because he had told them.

> **D' [People's words]** [11] So they said to him, "What should we do to you that the sea may become calm for us?"-- for the sea was becoming increasingly stormy.

C' [Jonah's words] [12] He said to them,

"Pick me up and throw me into the sea. Then the sea will become calm for you, for I know that on account of me this great storm *has come* upon you."

B' [13] However, the men rowed *desperately* to return to land but they could not, for the seas becoming *even* stormier against them. [14] Then they called on the LORD and said, "We earnestly pray, O LORD, **do not let us perish on account of this man's life and do not put innocent blood on us;** for You, O LORD, have done as You have pleased."

A' [15] So they picked up Jonah, threw him into the sea, and the **sea stopped its raging**. [16] Then the men feared the LORD greatly, and they offered a sacrifice to the LORD and made vows.

[God's response to Jonah's running away] [17] And the LORD appointed a great fish to swallow Jonah, and Jonah was in the stomach of the fish three days and three nights.

Discussion

The book of Jonah begins like other books of the prophets, saying that the word of the LORD came to Jonah. The first two verses were commands from the LORD. The third verse is Jonah's response to the LORD. The rest of the chapter is a chiasm which tells us that Jonah was fleeing from the LORD. The last verse is an action of the LORD in response to Jonah's running away.

Questioning the Passage

1. Who was Jonah? (v. 1)

Jonah the prophet is mentioned in 2 Kings. He lived and prophesied during the reign of King Jeroboam[4] son of Joash. "The Sages identify Jonah as the prophet sent by Elijah to anoint Yehu[5] as King of the Ten tribes (2 Kings 9:1). Pirkei DeRabbi Eliezer[6] identifies Jonah as a child whom Elijah revived (1 Kings 17).

---

[4] When Rehoboam convened Israel at Shechem, after his father's death, to confirm his own succession to the throne, Jeroboam, apprised of what had occurred, returned. He seems to have been the spokesman for assembled Israel and to have represented their demands for relief from the "grievous yoke." Upon the refusal of Rehoboam to accede to their demands, and the failure of the attempt to coerce the complainants into submission, which led to the stoning of Adoram, the ten northern tribes asserted their independence by proclaiming Jeroboam their king, the prophet Shemaiah preventing any warlike measures on the part of Rehoboam (I Kings xii. 1-24; II Chron. x., xi. 1-4). Source: JEROBOAM - JewishEncyclopedia.com. Accessed December 22, 2016.

[5] Son of Jehoshaphat and grandson of Nimshi, founder of the fifth Israelitish dynasty (842-743 B.C.); died 815 B.C., in the twenty-eighth year of his reign. Source: Jehu - JewishEncyclopedia.com. Accessed December 22, 2016.

[6] Haggadic midrashic work on Genesis, part of Exodus, and a few sentences of Numbers; ascribed to R. Eliezer b. Hyrcanus, and composed in Italy shortly after 833. Source: JewishEncyclopedia.com. Accessed December 22, 2016.

According to a tradition cited by Abarbanel[7], Jonah lived over 120 years.

2. Is anything known of Jonah's father, Amittai? (v. 2)

"Father of the prophet Jonah (II Kings, xiv. 25; Jonah, i. 1). According to rabbinical sources (Yer. Suk. v. 55*a*; Gen. R. xcviii.; Yalḳ., Jonah, § 550) Amittai came from the tribe of Zebulon and lived at Zarephath. There is a tradition that the widow who sustained the prophet Elijah there (I Kings, xvii. 9-24) was Amittai's wife, and that the child whom Elijah revived was Jonah (Pirḳe R. El. xxxiii.)."[8]

3. What is the significance of the city of

---

[7] **A**brabanel (Abravanel). Isaac ben Judah (1437–1508), Jewish statesman, commentator, and philosopher.. Source: Bowker, John. "Isaac Abravanel." In *The Concise Oxford Dictionary of World Religions*. Oxford: Oxford University Press, 2005.

[8] JewishEncyclopedia.com. Accessed December 22, 2016.

Nineveh? (v. 2)

The city of Nineveh was the capital of the Assyrian Empire.

4. Why does the Scriptures say that the city of Nineveh was a great city? (v. 2)

During the height of the Empire the city is believed to have had population that exceeded 120,000 people, making it an enormous city for its time.

5. Why had the wickedness of the city of Nineveh risen to the LORD? (v. 2)

There are several reasons the LORD was concerned about the wickedness of the city of Nineveh. According to Ibn Ezra[9], one reason offered was that the people of the city of Nineveh did not worship idols.

---

[9] Scholar and writer; born 1089-1167; died Jan. 28. Source: JewishEncyclopedia.com. Accessed December 22, 2016.

Rather, their wickedness was limited to moral and social sins. Therefore, God had compassion for them and gave the people an opportunity to repent.

According to Radak[10], another possibility is that the sin of Nineveh was in robbery and oppression, thus paralleling the evils of the generation of the flood and the Sodomites. This form of behavior destroyed the social order and therefore, since God wanted to preserve his creation, he intervened.

According to Malbim[11], another reason is that God intended to raise Assyria to

---

[10] Rabbi at Corfu, and later at Patros, Greece, at the beginning of the sixteenth century. **Source:** JewishEncyclopedia.com. Accessed April 3, 3017

[11] Russian rabbi, preacher, and Hebraist; born at Volochisk, Volhynia, in 1809; died at Kiev Sept. 18, 1879. The name "Malbim" is derived from the initials of his name (מלבים). Source: JewishEncyclopedia.com. Accessed December 22, 2016.

punish the Northern Kingdom of Israel because of the Northern Kingdom's sins. Therefore, God sent Jonah to Nineveh so that the people of Nineveh could repent and become worthy of their future mission.

6. Why did Jonah decide to flee to Tarshish? (v. 3)

Jonah fled to Tarshish so that he would not have to bring God's message to the Ninevites. For if the Ninevites had repented and God would have forgiven them, Jonah could have rationalized that he would be condemning Israel, who constantly ignored the prophetic call for repentance.

According to the Sages, Jonah probably had two concerns: (1) if the Ninevites would have repented and God would have spared them, he might have poured his wrath out against Israel for not having similarly repented in the face of repeated divine expectations; and (2) the survivors of the Assyrian attack could have accused him of prophesying falsely, resulting in Jonah profaning the name of God.

Perhaps Jonah the prophet may have been opposed to forgiveness after repentance. It is written in the Talmud, what is the sinner's punishment? If the LORD forgave the Ninevites for their sin, then what would have been their punishment?[12]

7. What is the significance of the city of Tarshish? (v. 3)

---

[12] Scherman, Nosson, Meir Zlotowitz, Sheah Brander, and Menachem Davis. "Jonah." In The Prophets: The Later Prophets with a Commentary Anthologized from the Rabbinic Writings. Brooklyn, NY: Mesorah Publications, 2013. p. 225.

The city of Tarshish was in the south of Spain, therefore it was a long way from Israel. In those days, people believed the LORD could not reach them once they left the land of Israel because they believed the LORD only lived in the land of Israel while on earth.

If Jonah believed the LORD could not reach him, why would he think the LORD could reach Nineveh? An answer is that Jonah could have thought that the LORD could not reach him when he was outside of Israel, but that the LORD could reach the Gentiles in Nineveh.

8. Why is the city of Tarshish repeated three times in verse three? (v. 3)

Repetition is used in the Hebrew Scriptures to emphasize a point. Jonah was running away from the LORD as fast as he could and as far away from the LORD as he could.

9. Why does verse four say that the LORD hurled a great wind and then a great storm? Does a great storm imply a great wind, if so, why the repetition?

The Scripture says that the LORD hurled a great wind and then a great storm tells us that natural occurrences did not bring the storm about, but that it was God who brought the storm. That would account for the repetition.[13]

10. Why did the men decide to lighten the ship by throwing the cargo overboard? (v. 5)

Pirkei DeRabbi Eliezer 10:31 records that because of the ineffectiveness of the

---

[13] IBID. p. 227.

sailors' prayers to their own gods they threw their idols into the sea thus lightening the boat but more importantly showing the LORD that they did not believe in their idols anymore and believed in Jonah's God.[14]

11. How could Jonah sleep through this great wind and great storm? (v. 5)

An interpretation of this verse is that Jonah could not sleep, so he went into the hold of the ship where the sailors were praying to their gods because Jonah did not feel that he should call upon the LORD since he was running away from the LORD. When Jonah went into the hold of the ship, he expected to die.

12. Why did the captain of the ship ask Jonah

---

[14] IBID.

to call upon his God to save them? (v. 6)

Since it was clear to the sailors that calling upon their gods would not help their situation, they must have figured that it would not hurt to ask Jonah to call upon his God.

13. Why did the crew decide that one of the crew or passengers was causing the storm? (v. 7)

The crew needed to explain why this great storm was upon them. Since it was a divine storm, it must have been greater than any storm they had ever experienced. In ancient days, omens like these were interpreted as divine intervention. Therefore, either the crew or one passenger caused the storm.

14. Why did they ask him what country he was

from? (v. 8)

The sailors asked this question of Jonah to determine whether he had caused their problems.

15. Why did the men get frightened when they learned Jonah was running away from the presence of the LORD? (v. 10)

The men on the boat must have known something about the God of Israel. Since they determined Jonah was causing the storm and with their knowledge of the God of Israel, they became frightened because they probably knew that the LORD was after Jonah and that they could die because of Jonah's fleeing from the LORD.

16. Why did the men not immediately throw Jonah overboard, rather they tried to row

desperately to return to the land? (v. 13)

Perhaps they were trying not to sacrifice Jonah's life to satisfy the LORD. If they could have rowed to land and safety, they could have escaped the wrath of the LORD's storm and Jonah's life would have been spared.

Another idea is that the men wanted Jonah off their ship without killing him, so they would not feel guilty.

17. When the sailors called upon the LORD does that mean that they believed in the LORD? (v. 14)

Since they offered their prayers to their idols with no effect, they offered their prayers to the LORD. This does not show that they believed in the LORD and thus abandoned their idols, but it means that they included the LORD in their collection of gods.

Main/Center Point

What Jonah learned from this experience was that you cannot flee from God. For the people of Israel, this prophecy would have told them that the LORD God reigns all over the earth, not just in Israel and in Judah. The idea of monotheism was taking a firm shape. In order to have true monotheism, the belief that other nations have different gods then you have to be overcome. By the sailors throwing their idols overboard because their prayers to their idols did nothing, it is like saying that they believed in the one true God, which is the God of Israel.

Symbols

1. What is the symbolism of Jonah being

swallowed by the great fish and being in its stomach for three days and three nights? (v. 17)

It should be noted that in the Tanakh and the Septuagint that verse seventeen is actually a part of chapter two and is verse one of the chapter. The LORD chose a big fish to be God's agent and to act for God upon the earth by swallowing Jonah. God chose a fish that would be large enough to hold Jonah in his stomach. The LORD does not like to upset the natural order but works within the framework of nature which he set up.[15]

Three is a number used in the Scripture to denote divine intervention. Therefore, God did not intervene until the third day.

---

[15] IBID. p. 229.

People's names

1. אֲמִתַּי *Amittay* **Meaning:** 'true,' the father of Jonah

2. יוֹנָה *Yonah* **Meaning:** an Israeli prophet

Name of places

1. תַּרְשִׁישׁ *Tarshish* **Meaning:** a son of Javan, the name his descendants, and the name of their land, also a port on the Mediterranean, and a city in Spain.

2. יָפוֹ *Yapho* or יָפוֹא *Yapho* **Meaning:** a seaport city of Israel

Word Study

1. קָרָא *qara* **Meaning:** *to call, proclaim, read* (v. 2)

   ^{NAU} **Genesis 1:5** God **called** the light day,

and the darkness He called night. And there was evening and there was morning, one day. (Gen. 1:5 NAU)

^{NAU} **Genesis 1:8** God **called** the expanse heaven. And there was evening and there was morning, a second day. (Gen. 1:8 NAU)

^{NAU} **Isaiah 22:12** Therefore in that day the LORD GOD of hosts **called** *you* to weeping, to wailing, To shaving the head and to wearing sackcloth (Isa. 22:12 NAU)

From the Theological Wordbook of the Old Testament: "The verb may represent the specification of a name. Naming is sometimes an assertion of sovereignty over the thing named. God's creating entailed naming and numbering the stars (Psa 147:4), the darkness (Gen 1:5), indeed all things (Isa 40:26). God presented the animals to Adam to assert his relative sovereignty over them (Gen 2:19). God sovereignly called Cyrus by name (note that election to a task is involved here, Isa 45:4).

Conclusion: Based on the meaning and usage of the word, the meaning "to call" is the better translation. Jonah was told by the LORD to go to Nineveh and to call out their sins. Jonah was to name the sins of the people. Probably the people did not know that what they were doing was sinful to the LORD. Jonah called out their sins and identified them for them.

Scripture cross references

Verse 1 2Ki 14:25; Mat 12:39-41; Mat 16:4; Luk 11:29, Luk 11:30, 32

Verse 3 Isa 23:1, Isa 23:6, 10; Jer 10:9; Gen 4:16; Psa 139:7, Psa 139:9, 10; Jos 19:46; 2Ch 2:16; Ezr 3:7; Act 9:36, Act 9:43

Verse 4 Psa 107:23-28; Psa 135:6, Psa 135:7

Verse 5 1Ki 18:26; Act 27:18, Act 27:19, 38

Verse 6 Psa 107:28; 2Sa 12:22; Amo 5:15

Verse 7 Jos 7:14-18; 1Sa 10:20, 1Sa 10:21; 1Sa 14:41, 1Sa 14:42; Act 1:23-26; Num 32:23; Pro 16:33

Verse 8 Jos 7:19; 1Sa 14:43; Gen 47:3; 1Sa 30:13

Verse 12   2Sa 24:17; 1Ch 21:17

Verse 17   Mat 12:40; Mat 16:4

Culture Section

Discussion

"The word of the LORD came to me" was one of the various ways used by the prophets to tell us that the LORD gave the prophet a vision. There are several other ways that prophets let us know that they had a vision. "The word of the LORD came to me" means "I was in a trance state or asleep and saw visions, I prophesied, I transcended the material world and was communing with God who is Spirit."[16]

Questioning the passage

1. Did Jonah believe that he could escape from the presence of the LORD

   There was the belief of a localized presence of the LORD which was in Israel and Judah. Even though the Hebrews

---

[16] Errico, Rocco A., and George M. Lamsa. *Aramaic Light on Ezekiel, Daniel, and the Minor Prophets: A Commentary Based on the Aramaic Language and Ancient Near Eastern Customs.* p. 159.

believed in the one and only true God, they did believe that the essence of the LORD resided in the Promised Land. Therefore, Jonah must have believed, even though the LORD is God and the essence of the LORD was in the Promised Land, that running away from the Promised Land might allow him to escape the LORD's directive.

2. How are lots cast in Jonah's day? (v. 7)

"Means of determining chances. Primitive peoples, and occasionally those on a higher plane of culture, resort to lots for the purposes of augury. They spin a coconut or entangle strips of leather in order to obtain an omen. Thieves especially are detected by the casting of lots, etc. (Tylor, "Primitive Culture," German ed., i. 78-82). The pagans on a ship with Jonah under stress of a storm cast lots in order to find out who among them had incurred the Divine anger (Jonah i. 7). Haman resorted to the lot when he intended to destroy the Jews (Esth. iii. 7). The Greek heroes cast their lots into Agamemnon's helmet in order to ascertain who should fight with Hector ("Iliad," vii. 171). In ancient Italy oracles with carved lots were used. "[17]

Thoughts

Through this part of the Jonah story, we learn the LORD is omnipresent on Earth. For us today, we already know that. For the people in Jonah's time, they did not know this. Jonah learned one cannot escape the LORD. The command Jonah was given upset him so much that he fled from the Promised Land.

------

[17] LOTS - JewishEncyclopedia.com. Accessed December 22, 2016.

The LORD followed Jonah by placing His breath (ruach) upon the waters and brought a great storm. In order to save the crew and passengers, Jonah had himself thrown overboard. It was a generous offer that he made. The last verse in the English versions concerns the large fish that the LORD brought up to swallow Jonah. In the Hebrew versions this last verse is the first verse of the next chapter.

Jonah Chapter Two

New American Standard 1995	Hebrew	Septuagint
[1] Then Jonah prayed to the LORD his God from the stomach of the fish, [2] and he said, "I called out of my distress to the LORD, And He answered me.	[1] וַיְמַ֤ן יְהוָה֙ דָּ֣ג גָּד֔וֹל לִבְלֹ֖עַ אֶת־יוֹנָ֑ה וַיְהִ֤י יוֹנָה֙ בִּמְעֵ֣י הַדָּ֔ג שְׁלֹשָׁ֥ה יָמִ֖ים וּשְׁלֹשָׁ֥ה לֵילֽוֹת׃ [2] וַיִּתְפַּלֵּ֣ל יוֹנָ֔ה אֶל־יְהוָ֖ה אֱלֹהָ֑יו	[1] Now the Lord had commanded a great whale to swallow up Jonas: and Jonas was in the belly of the whale three days and three nights.

New American Standard 1995	Hebrew	Septuagint
I cried for help from the depth of Sheol; You heard my voice. 3 "For You had cast me into the deep, Into the heart of the seas, And the current engulfed me. All Your	מִמְּעֵי הַדָּגָה: 3 וַיֹּאמֶר קָרָאתִי לִי מִצָּרָה אֶל־יְהוָה וַיַּעֲנֵנִי מִבֶּטֶן שְׁאוֹל שִׁוַּעְתִּי שָׁמַעְתָּ קוֹלִי: 4 וַתַּשְׁלִיכֵנִי מְצוּלָה בִּלְבַב יַמִּים וְנָהָר	2 And Jonas prayed to the Lord his God out of the belly of the whale, 3 and said, I cried in my affliction to the Lord my God, and he hearkened to me, *even* to my cry out of the belly

New American Standard 1995	Hebrew	Septuagint
breakers and billows passed over me. 4 "So I said, 'I have been expelled from Your sight. Nevertheless I will look again toward Your holy temple.' 5 "Water encompassed	יְסֹבְבֵ֑נִי כָּל־מִשְׁבָּרֶ֛יךָ וְגַלֶּ֖יךָ עָלַ֥י עָבָֽרוּ׃ 5 וַאֲנִ֣י אָמַ֔רְתִּי נִגְרַ֖שְׁתִּי מִנֶּ֣גֶד עֵינֶ֑יךָ אַ֚ךְ אוֹסִ֣יף לְהַבִּ֔יט אֶל־הֵיכַ֖ל קָדְשֶֽׁךָ׃ 6 אֲפָפ֤וּנִי מַ֙יִם֙ עַד־נֶ֔פֶשׁ תְּה֖וֹם	of hell: thou heardest my voice. 4 Thou didst cast me into the depths of the heart of the sea, and the floods compassed me: all thy billows and thy waves have passed

New American Standard 1995	Hebrew	Septuagint
me to the point of death. The great deep engulfed me, Weeds were wrapped around my head. 6 "I descended to the roots of the mountains. The earth	יְסֹבְבֵ֫נִי ס֥וּף חָב֖וּשׁ לְרֹאשִֽׁי: 7 לְקִצְבֵ֤י הָרִים֙ יָרַ֔דְתִּי הָאָ֛רֶץ בְּרִחֶ֥יהָ בַעֲדִ֖י לְעוֹלָ֑ם וַתַּ֧עַל מִשַּׁ֛חַת חַיַּ֖י יְהוָ֥ה אֱלֹהָֽי: 8 בְּהִתְעַטֵּ֤ף עָלַי֙ נַפְשִׁ֔י אֶת־יְהוָ֖ה	upon me. 5 And I said, I am cast out of thy presence: shall I indeed look again toward thy holy temple? 6 Water was poured around me to the soul:

New American Standard 1995	Hebrew	Septuagint
with its bars *was* around me forever, But You have brought up my life from the pit, O LORD my God. 7 "While I was fainting away, I remembered the LORD, And my	זָכַ֑רְתִּי וַתָּב֣וֹא אֵלֶ֨יךָ֙ תְּפִלָּתִ֔י אֶל־הֵיכַ֖ל קָדְשֶֽׁךָ׃ 9 מְשַׁמְּרִ֖ים הַבְלֵי־שָׁ֑וְא חַסְדָּ֖ם יַעֲזֹֽבוּ׃ 10 וַאֲנִ֗י בְּק֤וֹל תּוֹדָה֙ אֶזְבְּחָה־לָּ֔ךְ	the lowest deep compassed me, my head went down 7 to the clefts of the mountains; I went down into the earth, whose bars are the everlasting barriers: yet, O Lord my

New American Standard 1995	Hebrew	Septuagint
prayer came to You, Into Your holy temple. 8 "Those who regard vain idols Forsake their faithfulness, 9 But I will sacrifice to You With the voice of thanksgiving.	אֲשֶׁר נָדַרְתִּי אֲשַׁלֵּמָה יְשׁוּעָתָה לַיהוָה: ס 11 וַיֹּאמֶר יְהוָה לַדָּג וַיָּקֵא אֶת־יוֹנָה אֶל־הַיַּבָּשָׁה: פ	God, let my ruined life be restored. 8 When my soul was failing me, I remembered the Lord; and may my prayer come to thee into thy holy temple. 9 They that

New American Standard 1995	Hebrew	Septuagint
That which I have vowed I will pay. Salvation is from the LORD." 10 Then the LORD commanded the fish, and it vomited Jonah up onto the dry land.		observe vanities and lies have forsaken their own mercy. 10 But I will sacrifice to thee with the voice of praise and thanksgiving: all that I have vowed I will pay to

New American Standard 1995	Hebrew	Septuagint
		thee, the Lord of *my* salvation. [11] And the whale was commanded by the Lord, and it cast up Jonas on the dry *land*.

Process of Discovery

Linguistics Section

Linguistic Structure

A (1:17)And the LORD appointed **a great fish to swallow Jonah**, and Jonah was in the stomach of the fish three days and three nights.

B [1] Then Jonah prayed to the LORD his God from the stomach of the fish, [2] and he said, "I called out of my distress to the LORD, And He answered me. **I cried for help from the depth of Sheol**; You heard my voice.

C [3] "For You had cast me into the deep, Into the heart of the seas, And the current engulfed me. All Your breakers and billows passed over me. [4] "So I said, 'I have been expelled from Your sight. Nevertheless I will look again toward Your holy temple.' [5] "Water encompassed me to the point of death. The great deep engulfed me,

Weeds were wrapped around my head.

B' [6] "I descended to the roots of the mountains. The earth with its bars *was* around me forever, **But You have brought up my life from the pit**, O LORD my God. [7] "While I was fainting away, I remembered the LORD, And my prayer came to You, Into Your holy temple. [8] "Those who regard vain idols Forsake their faithfulness, [9] But I will sacrifice to You With the voice of thanksgiving. That which I have vowed I will pay. Salvation is from the LORD."

A' [10] Then the LORD commanded the **fish, and it vomited Jonah up** onto the dry land.

Discussion

In the New American Standard 1995 version of the Bible, the verse about Jonah being swallowed by the big fish is in chapter one. In several other versions of the Scriptures, this verse is a part of chapter two. For the completeness of the chiasm in chapter two it is necessary to include verse 1:17 in this chapter. The chiasm begins with Jonah being swallowed by the Great Fish, and it ends with the Great Fish spitting out Jonah.

Questioning the Passage

1. How could Jonah have survived in the belly of a fish for three days? (v. 1:17)

   The large fish which swallowed Jonah was acting as an agent of the LORD. Normally, Jonah could not have survived the belly of the fish for three days. However, he could survive because God wanted him to survive. If Jonah was in the belly of the fish, he would have lasted about one hour, if that much, because he would have run out of oxygen. Jonah surviving for three days symbolically tells us he drowned and died and was reborn three days later. One can say that Jonah died to his old self, the self that ran away from the commandments of the LORD, and was reborn as a faithful disciple of the LORD. He experienced a transformation.

2. Why is the belly of the fish called Sheol in verse 2?

The belly of the fish is called Sheol to correspond with the symbolism that Jonah died and was reborn. This also could tell us that those who do not obey the commands of the LORD will go to Sheol. Jonah probably thought he was going to die when the big fish swallowed him.

3. What are the LORD's breakers and billows? (v. 3)

The Hebrew for "breakers and billows" can both be translated as waves. Therefore, there is a repetition within the verse telling us that Jonah was actually sinking because the waves of the sea were covering him, and because it is repeated with a synonym, it gives it a stronger emphasis.

4. What does it mean to look toward the Holy Temple? (v. 4)

To look toward the holy temple, in Jonah's day, meant to offer prayers to the LORD.

5. What is the symbolism of having weeds wrapped around Jonah's head? (v. 5)

There is no symbolism about the weeds wrapped around Jonah's head. This is just another emphasis that Jonah was thrown into the sea.

6. What are the bars of the earth? (v. 6)

No information on this expression has yet been found. The Midrash would have to be explored.

7. What is the meaning of verses 8 & 9?

These two verses refer to people who were idol worshipers. It is also possible that these verses refer to the sailors who did not believe in the LORD. It is a part of the prayer Jonah offered to the LORD which reminded him he must place his trust in the LORD and not in other idols or false gods. Jonah acknowledges that salvation only comes from the LORD.

Main/Center Point

Jonah came to understand that salvation comes only from the LORD. He also learned that he could not run away from the LORD and that he needed to obey the LORD's commandments that were laid out before him. We are also told that even if we openly disobey the LORD that the LORD will take us back as long as we will admit to our mistake and ask for forgiveness.

Symbols

1. What is the symbolism of the number three?

   The main symbolism of the number three is that it represents the LORD. It is emphasized in Christianity because of the Trinity doctrine.

2. What are the roots of the mountains? (v. 6)

   The roots of the mountains can also be translated as the base of the mountains, or the clefts of the mountain. The roots of the mountain could be symbolic of Jonah not wanting to heed the commands of the LORD. The Temple existed on the top of

Mount Sinai. Since ancient people believed that the closer you could get to the firmament, the closer you could get to God, going to the roots of the mountain would get you as far away from God as possible.

Translation Inconsistencies

The following is not a translation inconsistency, but is interesting, nevertheless. The Hebrew says that a male fish swallowed Jonah. However, when Jonah prayed to the LORD from inside the belly of the fish, the Hebrew says that it was a female fish. There is not a lot of data about why a male fish swallows Jonah and becomes a pregnant female fish. When the book of Jonah was written the people probably got a good chuckle out of it.

Ⱳᵀᵀ Jonah 2:1   וַיְמַן יְהוָה דָּג גָּדֹול לִבְלֹעַ אֶת־יֹונָה

וַיְהִי יֹונָה בִּמְעֵי הַדָּג שְׁלֹשָׁה יָמִים וּשְׁלֹשָׁה לֵילֹות׃

Ⱳᵀᵀ Jonah 2:2   וַיִּתְפַּלֵּל יֹונָה אֶל־יְהוָה אֱלֹהָיו

מִמְּעֵי הַדָּגָה׃

Jonah 2:10   וַיֹּאמֶר יְהוָה לַדָּג וַיָּקֵא אֶת־יֹונָה

אֶל־הַיַּבָּשָׁה׃

People's names

1. יֹונָה *Yonah*   **Meaning:** an Israeli

prophet

Scripture cross references

Verse 2 1Sa 30:6; Psa 18:4-6; Psa 22:24; Psa

120:1; Psa 18:5, Psa 18:6; Psa 86:13;

Psa 88:1-7

Verse 3 Psa 18:5; Psa 116:3; Isa 38:10; Mat 16:18; Job 33:28; Psa 16:10; Psa 30:3; Isa 38:17

Verse 9 Psa 50:14, Psa 50:23; Jer 33:11; Hos 14:2; Job 22:27; Ecc 5:4, Ecc 5:5; Psa 3:8; Isa 45:1

Culture Section

Discussion

Jonah makes a vow while in the fish's belly. Semitic tradition was that if you made a vow, especially to the LORD, then you carried it out no matter how long it took and no matter how many resources it took.

Thoughts

Jonah ran from the LORD because he did not want to do what the LORD had commanded. In this chapter, we learn of God's forgiveness and salvation. Jonah offered his prayers to the LORD admitting to his mistake in telling the LORD that he would obey him faithfully. Because of this admission of guilt and repentance the LORD saved Jonah by having a large fish spit him out on land. Somewhere in most people's lives they reject what the LORD God has to offer them. However, God will not allow people to just go into the abyss but rather God will allow us to return into a relationship of discipleship with him. Therefore, we see in this chapter the love God has for each and every one of us.

Jonah Chapter Three

New American Standard 1995	Hebrew	Septuagint
[1] Now the word of the LORD came to Jonah the second time, saying, [2] "Arise, go to Nineveh the great city and proclaim to it the proclamation	וַיְהִ֧י [1] דְבַר־יְהוָ֛ה אֶל־יוֹנָ֖ה שֵׁנִ֥ית לֵאמֹֽר: [2] ק֛וּם לֵ֥ךְ אֶל־נִֽינְוֵ֖ה הָעִ֣יר הַגְּדוֹלָ֑ה וּקְרָ֤א אֵלֶ֙יהָ֙ אֶת־הַקְּרִיאָ֔ה אֲשֶׁ֥ר אָנֹכִ֖י דֹּבֵ֥ר	And the word of the Lord came to Jonas the second time, saying, [2] Rise, go to Nineve, the great city, and preach in it according to

New American Standard 1995	Hebrew	Septuagint
which I am going to tell you." 3 So Jonah arose and went to Nineveh according to the word of the LORD. Now Nineveh was an exceedingly great city, a three days'	אֵלֶיךָ׃ 3 וַיָּקָם יוֹנָה וַיֵּלֶךְ אֶל־נִינְוֵה כִּדְבַר יְהוָה וְנִינְוֵה הָיְתָה עִיר־גְּדוֹלָה לֵאלֹהִים מַהֲלַךְ שְׁלֹשֶׁת יָמִים׃ 4 וַיָּחֶל יוֹנָה לָבוֹא בָעִיר	the former preaching which I spoke to thee of. 3 And Jonas arose, and went to Nineve, as the Lord had spoken. Now Nineve was an exceeding great city, of

New American Standard 1995	Hebrew	Septuagint
walk. ⁴ Then Jonah began to go through the city one day's walk; and he cried out and said, "Yet forty days and Nineveh will be overthrown." ⁵ Then the people of	מַהֲלַךְ יוֹם אֶחָד וַיִּקְרָא וַיֹּאמַר עוֹד אַרְבָּעִים יוֹם וְנִינְוֵה נֶהְפָּכֶת: ⁵ וַיַּאֲמִינוּ אַנְשֵׁי נִינְוֵה בֵּאלֹהִים וַיִּקְרְאוּ־צוֹם וַיִּלְבְּשׁוּ שַׂקִּים מִגְּדוֹלָם וְעַד־קְטַנָּם:	about three days' journey. ⁴ And Jonas began to enter into the city about a day's journey, and he proclaimed, and said, Yet three days, and Nineve shall be

New American Standard 1995	Hebrew	Septuagint
Nineveh believed in God; and they called a fast and put on sackcloth from the greatest to the least of them. ⁶ When the word reached the king of Nineveh, he arose from his throne,	⁶ וַיִּגַּע הַדָּבָר אֶל־מֶלֶךְ נִינְוֵה וַיָּקָם מִכִּסְאוֹ וַיַּעֲבֵר אַדַּרְתּוֹ מֵעָלָיו וַיְכַס שַׂק וַיֵּשֶׁב עַל־הָאֵפֶר׃ ⁷ וַיַּזְעֵק וַיֹּאמֶר בְּנִינְוֵה מִטַּעַם הַמֶּלֶךְ וּגְדֹלָיו לֵאמֹר הָאָדָם	overthrown. ⁵ And the men of Nineve believed God, and proclaimed a fast, and put on sackcloths, from the greatest of them to the least of

New American Standard 1995	Hebrew	Septuagint
laid aside his robe from him, covered *himself* with sackcloth and sat on the ashes. 7 He issued a proclamation and it said, "In Nineveh by the decree of the king and his nobles: Do	וְהַבְּהֵמָ֖ה הַבָּקָ֑ר וְהַצֹּ֔אן אַל־יִטְעֲמוּ֙ מְא֔וּמָה אַל־יִרְע֔וּ וּמַ֖יִם אַל־יִשְׁתּֽוּ׃ 8 וְיִתְכַּסּ֣וּ שַׂקִּ֗ים הָֽאָדָם֙ וְהַבְּהֵמָ֔ה וְיִקְרְא֥וּ אֶל־אֱלֹהִ֖ים בְּחָזְקָ֑ה וְיָשֻׁ֗בוּ	them. 6 And the word reached the king of Nineve, and he arose from off his throne, and took off his raiment from him, and put on sackcloth, and sat on

New American Standard 1995	Hebrew	Septuagint
not let man, beast, herd, or flock taste a thing. Do not let them eat or drink water. 8 "But both man and beast must be covered with sackcloth; and let men call on God earnestly that	אִישׁ מִדַּרְכּוֹ הָרָעָה וּמִן־הֶחָמָס אֲשֶׁר בְּכַפֵּיהֶם: 9 מִי־יוֹדֵעַ יָשׁוּב וְנִחַם הָאֱלֹהִים וְשָׁב מֵחֲרוֹן אַפּוֹ וְלֹא נֹאבֵד: 10 וַיַּרְא הָאֱלֹהִים	ashes. 7 And proclamation was made, and it was commanded in Nineve by the king an by his great men, saying, Let not men, or cattle, or oxen, or sheep, taste *any thing*, nor

New American Standard 1995	Hebrew	Septuagint
each may turn from his wicked way and from the violence which is in his hands. ⁹ "Who knows, God may turn and relent and withdraw His burning anger so that we will not	אֶת־מַעֲשֵׂיהֶם כִּי־שָׁבוּ מִדַּרְכָּם הָרָעָה וַיִּנָּחֶם הָאֱלֹהִים עַל־הָרָעָה אֲשֶׁר־דִּבֶּר לַעֲשׂוֹת־לָהֶם וְלֹא עָשָׂה׃	feed, nor drink water. ⁸ So men and cattle were clothed with sackcloths, and cried earnestly to God; and they turned every one from their evil way, and from the

New American Standard 1995	Hebrew	Septuagint
perish." [10] When God saw their deeds, that they turned from their wicked way, then God relented concerning the calamity which He had declared He would bring upon them.		iniquity that was in their hands, saying, [9] Who knows if God will repent, and turn from his fierce anger, and *so* we shall not perish? [10] And God

New American Standard 1995	Hebrew	Septuagint
And He did not do *it*.		saw their works, that they turned from their evil ways; and God repented of the evil which he had said he would do to them; and he did *it* not.

Process of Discovery

Linguistics Section

Linguistic Structure

[Action] [1] Now the word of the LORD came to Jonah the second time, saying, [2] "Arise, go to Nineveh the great city and proclaim to it the proclamation which I am going to tell you."

[Reaction] [3] So Jonah arose and went to Nineveh according to the word of the LORD. Now Nineveh was an exceedingly great city, a three days' walk. [4] Then Jonah began to go through the city one day's walk; and he cried out and said, "Yet forty days and Nineveh will be overthrown."

[Action] [5] Then the people of Nineveh believed in God; and they called a fast and put on sackcloth from the greatest to the least of them.

[Continuing Action] [6] When the word reached the king of Nineveh, he arose from his throne, laid aside his robe from him, covered *himself* with sackcloth and sat on the ashes. [7] He issued a proclamation and it said, "In Nineveh by the decree of the king and his nobles: Do not let man, beast, herd, or flock taste a thing. Do not let them eat or drink water.

[Continuing Action] [8] "But both man and beast must be covered with sackcloth; and let men call on God earnestly that each may turn from his wicked way and from the violence which is in his hands.

[Anticipated reaction][9] "Who knows, God may turn and relent and withdraw His burning anger so that we will not perish."

[Reaction] [10] When God saw their deeds, that they turned from their wicked way, then God relented concerning the calamity which He had declared He would bring upon them. And He did not do *it*.

Discussion

This chapter consists of two actions and two reactions. The first action was the LORD instructing Jonah to go to Ninevah and give them the message of the need for their repentance. The second action is that the people repented, which eventually extended to the king. The king of Ninevah hoped the LORD would forgive them.

Questioning the Passage

1. Why is Ninevah called the great city? (v. 2)

The city of Ninevah was great because of the size of the city. In ancient days, it was difficult to have a large city unless there was plenty of water and land available.

2. What is the significance of it being a three-day walk for Jonah to get to Ninevah? (v. 3)

The Talmud in Pesachim 93b estimates that a human can walk 10 parsas a day, which is approximately 26 miles. Therefore, Jonah was 78 miles from the city.[18]

3. Why was the city of Ninevah called an exceeding great city? (v. 3)

וְנִינְוֵה הָיְתָה עִיר־גְּדוֹלָה לֵאלֹהִים (Jon. 3:3 WTT)

---

[18] Scherman, Nosson, and Meir Zlotowitz. "Chapter 3. Jonah" In *Jonah: The Later Prophets with a Commentary Antholigized from the Rabbinic Writings.* Brooklyn, N.Y: Mesorah Publications, 2014. p. 232.

"The translation *enormously great* follows Radak, who explains that when Scriptures wishes to emphasize size or importance, it idiomatically attaches God's name to the noun."[19] The word *El* or *Elohim* are used, not the actual name of God.

---

[19] IBID, p. 233.

4. What is the significance that Ninevah was a one day walk in size? (v. 4)

This tells us that Ninevah could have been a city of 26 miles in diameter. It was a huge city which corresponds to the language of it being an enormous city. This conclusion comes from reading verse four that it took Jonah one day to walk through the city.

Main/Center Point

Jonah had decided to follow the Word of the LORD. He goes to the city of Ninevah and was probably shocked to see the people mourning for their sins. The sackcloth and fasting is a sign of repentance. When the King of Ninevah heard the words of Jonah and that his people were in repentance, he joined them. The King must have heard Jonah's word through his advisor because the Bible does not say Jonah ever met the King.

People's names

1. יוֹנָה *Yonah* (402a) **Meaning:** an Israeli prophet

Name of places

1. נִינְוֵה *Nineveh* **Meaning:** capital of Assyria

Scripture cross references

Verse 4 Mat 12:41; Luk 11:32

Verse 5 Dan 9:3; Joe 1:14

Verse 6 Est 4:1-4; Jer 6:26; Eze 27:30, Eze 27:3

Verse 7 2Ch 20:3; Ezr 8:21;

Verse 8 Psalm 130:1; 2Ch 20:3; Ezr 8:21;

Verse 9 2Sa 12:22; Joe 2:14

Culture Section

Questioning the Passage

1. What is the cultural significance of sack cloth? (v. 5)

   Sack cloth and fasting is a sign of repentance. Sack cloth were garments made of goat hair. Over the years sack cloth became the name of clothing one wore when in mourning

2. What is the cultural significance that the king rose from his throne? (v. 6)

   The king rising from his throne is a sign of reverence to the LORD.

3. What is the cultural significance that the king issued a decree? (v. 7)

The decree of the king was the king showing his people his agreement with the decision to repent and believe in the LORD. It is interesting that in this case the King was willing to follow the will of his people.

Cultural Echoes

The number 40: 40 days of rain with Noah, 40 years of Israel in the desert, Isaac was 40 years old when he married Rebekah, Esau was 40 years old when he married, Jacob presented 40 cows to Esau, 40 days to embalm Jacob when he died in Egypt, Moses was on Mt. Sinai for 40 days, the spies Moses sent into Caanan were there for 40 days, Joshua was 40 years old when Moses sent him as a spy into Caanan, forty year cycles in Judges, and a lot more.

Culture and Linguistics Section

Discussion

What is interesting is that the name of the LORD is not mentioned in this chapter. Elohim is used in the verses that speak about the people of Nineveh. The cultural understanding is that the name of the LORD is only for the Hebrews is shown here.

Thoughts

From the point of view that the book of Jonah is a prophecy, a problem occurs because history tells us that the Ninevites did not repent and when the Assyrian empire rose, with Nineveh being its capital, the people treated their enemies horribly. So many lives would have been spared from torture had the Assyrian empire never occurred. But it did occur. Therefore, another way to view the book of Jonah is to see it as a fictional book where the LORD allowed non-Hebrews to receive salvation if they repented of their evil and sins. Since the people of Israel believed for quite some time that the LORD was their God and only their God, the book of Jonah had to be a shock. In the understanding of the evolution of monotheism, Israel did not show signs of monotheism, one God for all people, until the book of Jonah was written. In this chapter we read that the LORD is God of all people.

Jonah Chapter Four

New American Standard 1995	Hebrew	Septuagint
¹But it greatly displeased Jonah and he became angry. ² He prayed to the LORD and said, "Please LORD, was not this what I said while I was still in my	¹וַיֵּ֥רַע אֶל־יוֹנָ֖ה רָעָ֣ה גְדוֹלָ֑ה וַיִּ֖חַר לֽוֹ: ²וַיִּתְפַּלֵּ֨ל אֶל־יְהוָ֜ה וַיֹּאמַ֗ר אָנָּ֤ה יְהוָה֙ הֲלוֹא־זֶ֣ה דְבָרִ֗י עַד־הֱיוֹתִי֙	But Jonas was very deeply grieved, and he was confounded. ² And he prayed to the Lord, and said, O Lord, were not these my words when I was

New American Standard 1995	Hebrew	Septuagint
own country? Therefore in order to forestall this I fled to Tarshish, for I knew that You are a gracious and compassionate God, slow to anger and abundant in lovingkindness, and one	עַל־אַדְמָתִי עַל־כֵּן קִדַּמְתִּי לִבְרֹחַ תַּרְשִׁישָׁה כִּי יָדַעְתִּי כִּי אַתָּה אֵל־חַנּוּן וְרַחוּם אֶרֶךְ אַפַּיִם וְרַב־חֶסֶד וְנִחָם	yet in my land? therefore I made haste to flee to Tharsis; because I knew that thou are merciful and compassionate, long-suffering, and abundant in kindness, and

New American Standard 1995	Hebrew	Septuagint
who relents concerning calamity. 3 "Therefore now, O LORD, please take my life from me, for death is better to me than life." 4 The LORD said, "Do you have good	עַל־הָרָעָה: 3 וְעַתָּה יְהוָֹה קַח־נָא אֶת־נַפְשִׁי מִמֶּנִּי כִּי טוֹב מוֹתִי מֵחַיָּי: ס 4 וַיֹּאמֶר יְהוָֹה הַהֵיטֵב חָרָה לָךְ: 5 וַיֵּצֵא יוֹנָה	repentest of evil. 3 And now, Lord God, take my life from me; for *it is* better for me to die than to live. 4 And the Lord said to Jonas, Art thou very much grieved?

New American Standard 1995	Hebrew	Septuagint
reason to be angry?" 5 Then Jonah went out from the city and sat east of it. There he made a shelter for himself and sat under it in the shade until he could see what would happen	מִן־הָעִיר וַיֵּשֶׁב מִקֶּדֶם לָעִיר וַיַּעַשׂ לוֹ שָׁם סֻכָּה וַיֵּשֶׁב תַּחְתֶּיהָ בַּצֵּל עַד אֲשֶׁר יִרְאֶה מַה־יִּהְיֶה בָּעִיר׃ ⁶וַיְמַן	5 And Jonas went out from the city, and sat over against the city; and he made for himself there a booth, and he sat under it, until he should perceive what would become of the city.

New American Standard 1995	Hebrew	Septuagint
in the city. 6 So the LORD God appointed a plant and it grew up over Jonah to be a shade over his head to deliver him from his discomfort. And Jonah was extremely happy about	יְהוָֽה־אֱלֹהִים קִיקָיוֹן וַיַּעַל ׀ מֵעַל לְיוֹנָה לִהְיוֹת צֵל עַל־רֹאשׁוֹ לְהַצִּיל לוֹ מֵרָעָתוֹ וַיִּשְׂמַח יוֹנָה עַל־הַקִּיקָיוֹן שִׂמְחָה	6 And the Lord God commanded a gourd, and it came up over the head of Jonas, to be a shadow over his head, to shade him from his calamities: and Jonas rejoiced with great joy for the gourd.

New American Standard 1995	Hebrew	Septuagint
the plant. ⁷ But God appointed a worm when dawn came the next day and it attacked the plant and it withered. ⁸ When the sun came up God appointed a scorching east	גְדוֹלָֽה׃ ⁷ וַיְמַ֣ן הָֽאֱלֹהִים֙ תּוֹלַ֔עַת בַּעֲל֥וֹת הַשַּׁ֖חַר לַֽמָּחֳרָ֑ת וַתַּ֥ךְ אֶת־הַקִּֽיקָי֖וֹן וַיִּיבָֽשׁ׃ ⁸ וַיְהִ֣י ׀ כִּזְרֹ֣חַ הַשֶּׁ֗מֶשׁ וַיְמַ֨ן	⁷ And God commanded a worm the next morning, and it smote the gourd, and it withered away. ⁸ And it came to pass at the rising of the sun, that God commanded a burning east wind; and the

New American Standard 1995	Hebrew	Septuagint
wind, and the sun beat down on Jonah's head so that he became faint and begged with *all* his soul to die, saying, "Death is better to me than life." ⁹ Then God said to Jonah, "Do you have	אֱלֹהִים רוּחַ קָדִים חֲרִישִׁית וַתַּ֣ךְ הַשֶּׁמֶשׁ עַל־רֹאשׁ יוֹנָה וַיִּתְעַלָּף וַיִּשְׁאַל אֶת־נַפְשׁוֹ לָמוּת וַיֹּאמֶר טוֹב מוֹתִי מֵחַיָּי׃	sun smote on the head of Jonas, and he fainted, and despaired of his life, and said, *It is* better for me to die than to live. ⁹ And God said to Jonas, Art thou very much grieved for the gourd?

New American Standard 1995	Hebrew	Septuagint
good reason to be angry about the plant?" And he said, "I have good reason to be angry, even to death." ¹⁰ Then the LORD said, "You had compassion on the plant for which you	⁹ וַיֹּ֣אמֶר אֱלֹהִים֙ אֶל־יוֹנָ֔ה הַהֵיטֵ֥ב חָרָה־לְךָ֖ עַל־הַקִּֽיקָי֑וֹן וַיֹּ֕אמֶר הֵיטֵ֥ב חָֽרָה־לִ֖י עַד־מָֽוֶת׃ ¹⁰ וַיֹּ֣אמֶר יְהֹוָ֔ה	And he said, I am very much grieved, even to death. ¹⁰ And the Lord said, Thou hadst pity on the gourd, for which thou has not suffered, neither didst thou rear it; which came

New American Standard 1995	Hebrew	Septuagint
did not work and *which* you did not cause to grow, which came up overnight and perished overnight. 11 "Should I not have compassion on Nineveh, the great city in which there are more than	אַתָּה חַסְתָּ עַל־הַקִּיקָיֹון אֲשֶׁר לֹא־עָמַלְתָּ בֹּו וְלֹא גִדַּלְתֹּו שֶׁבִּן־לַיְלָה הָיָה וּבִן־לַיְלָה אָבָד: 11 וַאֲנִי לֹא אָחוּס	up before night, and perished before *another* night: 11 and shall not I spare Nineve, the great city, in which dwell more than twelve myriads of human beings, who do not

New American Standard 1995	Hebrew	Septuagint
120,000 persons who do not know *the difference* between their right and left hand, as well as many animals?"	עַל־נִינְוֵה הָעִיר הַגְּדוֹלָה אֲשֶׁר יֶשׁ־בָּהּ הַרְבֵּה מִשְׁתֵּים־עֶשְׂרֵה רִבּוֹ אָדָם אֲשֶׁר לֹא־יָדַע בֵּין־יְמִינוֹ לִשְׂמֹאלוֹ וּבְהֵמָה רַבָּה׃	know their right hand or their left hand; and *also* much cattle?

New American Standard 1995	Hebrew	Septuagint

Process of Discovery

Linguistics Section

Linguistic Structure

A [1] **[Dissatisfaction of Jonah]** But it greatly displeased Jonah and he became angry. [2] He prayed to the LORD and said, "Please LORD, was not this what I said while I was still in my *own* country? Therefore in order to forestall this I fled to Tarshish, for I knew that You are a gracious and compassionate God, slow to anger and abundant in lovingkindness, and one who relents concerning calamity. [3] "Therefore now, O LORD, please take my life from me, for death is better to me than life."

B [4] The LORD said, "**Do you have good reason to be angry?**"

C [The LORD saves] [5] Then Jonah

went out from the city and sat east of it. There he made a shelter for himself and sat under it in the shade until he could see what would happen in the city. [6] So the LORD God appointed a plant and it grew up over Jonah to be a shade over his head to deliver him from his discomfort. And Jonah was extremely happy about the plant.

A' [7] **[Dissatisfaction of Jonah]** But God appointed a worm when dawn came the next day and it attacked the plant and it withered. [8] When the sun came up God appointed a scorching east wind, and the sun beat down on Jonah's head so that he became faint and begged with *all* his soul to die, saying, "Death is better to me than life."

B' [9] Then God said to Jonah, **"Do you have good reason to be angry about the**

plant?" And he said, "I have good reason to be angry, even to death."

C' [The LORD saves] [10] Then the LORD said, "You had compassion on the plant for which you did not work and *which* you did not cause to grow, which came up overnight and perished overnight. [11] "Should I not have compassion on Nineveh, the great city in which there are more than 120,000 persons who do not know *the difference* between their right and left hand, as well as many animals?"

Discussion

This chapter is a chiasm of A-B-C-A'-B'-C'. The A and C blocks are repetition because of their mutual topics. Block B is a linguistic repetition.

Questioning the Passage

1. Why was Jonah angry when the people of Nineveh listened to the Word of the LORD that Jonah brought? (v. 1)

   The people of Israel did not listen to the prophets, but the people of Nineveh did. Jonah was angry because the people did what the prophet said. The people did repent. Why would these aliens to the LORD's Word listen to the LORD while the LORD's people did not listen? It does appear to show a different level of trust and honor of the LORD and it was not from the children of Israel.

2. What did Jonah say in "his own country?" (v. 2)

The text does not have Jonah saying anything, but fleeing. This verse is referring to the event of Jonah fleeing from the Word of the LORD while he was in Israel. Jonah did not want to take a prophecy to a foreign people who were probably idol worshipers.[20]

3. Why did Jonah desire death? (v. 3)

Jonah might have known that Israel would not repent and that the Assyrians would eventually invade and destroy the ten northern tribes. Jonah preferred death rather than seeing his country destroyed and his people killed.

4. Why did the LORD have to ask Jonah

---

[20] Scherman, Nosson, and Meir Zlotowitz. "Chapter 3. Jonah" In *Jonah: The Later Prophets with a Commentary Antholigized from the Rabbinic Writings*. Brooklyn, N.Y: Mesorah Publications, 2014. p. 235.

about His anger? (v. 4)

This is a rhetorical question, implying that Jonah would yet be shown that his displeasure was improper (Rashi[21]).[22]

5. Is there a significance to Jonah sitting east of the city? (v. 5)

By sitting to the east of the city, the sun could shine upon him. It was safer to be on the east side of the city because the city gate of ancient cities were built on the east side. The gate would have soldiers there for defense of an enemy attack.

6. What is the symbolism of the plant that grew around Jonah? (v. 6)

---

[21] French commentator on Bible and Talmud; born at Troyes in 1040; died there July 13, 1105. His fame has made him the subject of many legends. Source: http://jewishencyclopedia.com

[22] IBID. p. 235

The plant is simply a divine gesture of the LORD to comfort Jonah in his distress.

7. Why did God take the plant away from Jonah? (v. 7)

The worm came in the morning to eat the plant just when Jonah needed it for its shade. Perhaps the LORD took the plant because it was given to him for comfort, yet Jonah remained angry at the events that had taken place in the city. Was Jonah angry with himself, or was he angry with his people? A prophet who cannot influence God's people but can influence the aliens is not a prophet of the LORD. This could be the reason for Jonah's distress.

The LORD has given the plant to cheer up Jonah. But Jonah did not let go of his anger. So, the LORD took the gift away.

8. What is the symbolism of the scorching east wind? (v. 8)

The wind is not a symbol, it is just an additional stress on Jonah. The sun and the wind would have made things uncomfortable for Jonah. This could be viewed as a punishment to Jonah for his attitude towards what the LORD wanted done. If one is truly a servant of the LORD, then one should not question how God works.

9. What is the comparison of Jonah's compassion for the plant and God's compassion for Nineveh? (v. 10 & 11)

Jonah had compassion for the plant that he did not plant nor cultivate. God was saying that He created the people of Nineveh and that He had compassion for them. This is a further example of how the Israelites needed to come to understand monotheism. The LORD was the God of all people. By sparing the people from death because of their evil ways, thus offering salvation, the LORD shows the Hebrews about the extent of the power of the LORD.

People's names

1. יוֹנָה *Yonah* **Meaning:** an Israeli prophet

Name of places

1. נִינְוֵה *Nineveh* **Meaning:** capital of Assyria

Word Study

1. סֻכָּה *sukkah* **Meaning:** *a thicket, booth*

^{NAU} **Leviticus 23:34** "Speak to the sons of Israel, saying, 'On the fifteenth of this seventh month is the Feast of **Booths** for seven days to the LORD. (Lev. 23:34 NAU)

^{NAU} **2 Samuel 11:11** Uriah said to David, "The ark and Israel and Judah are staying in temporary **shelters**, and my LORD Joab and

the servants of my LORD are camping in the open field. Shall I then go to my house to eat and to drink and to lie with my wife? By your life and the life of your soul, I will not do this thing." (2 Sam. 11:11 NAU)

^{NAU} **2 Samuel 22:12** "And He made darkness **canopies** around Him, A mass of waters, thick clouds of the sky. (2 Sam. 22:12 NAU)

^{NAU} **1 Kings 20:12** When *Ben-hadad* heard this message, as he was drinking with the kings in the temporary **shelters**, he said to his servants, "Station *yourselves*." So they stationed *themselves* against the city. (1 Ki. 20:12 NAU)

Conclusion

Sukkah is used in two manners in the Scripture. As the verses above indicate the word means "shelter." Jonah built himself a shelter because he could not find a place to sleep. Refer to the cultural section for more information. Jonah had traversed the city warning the people about the upcoming doom. It is possible that he did not want to stay in the city that evening. Therefore, since he slept that evening outside the city, to the east of the city, he needed to build himself a shelter.

^{NAU} **Leviticus 23:34** "Speak to the sons of Israel, saying, 'On the fifteenth of this seventh month is the Feast of Booths for seven days to the LORD. (Lev. 23:34 NAU)

This verse from Leviticus is one of many which refers to the Feast of Booths (Sukkot) in which the Hebrews built *Sukkot*, shelters out in the fields during the fall harvest. There is a debate as to whether or the reference about Sukkot is about the Festival or some other concern. Connecting the Jonah Sukkot would create an interesting midrash interpretation.

Scripture cross references

Verse 1 Mat 20:15; Luk 15:28

Verse 3 1Ki 19:4; Job 6:8, Job 6:9; Job 7:15, Job 7:16; Ecc 7:1

Verse 5 1Ki 19:9, 1Ki 19:13

Verse 8 Ezekiel 19:12; Hos 13:15; Psa 121:6; Isa 49:10

Culture Section

Discussion

When visitors came to a city and could not find a place to sleep, they would go outside of the city and sleep under a tree. Jonah went outside the city to sleep that night. He created a shelter and the LORD provided a tree for him to sleep under.[23]

Questioning the Passage

1. What does it mean not to know the difference between the right and left hand? (v. 11)

This is a Semitic idiom which means the person is too young to discern between good and evil. The left hand is evil while the right hand is good.[24]

2. What is the reference to the animals in verse ten?

"This figuratively refers to the adults who had beastlike sensibilities, inasmuch as they do not know their Creator (Rashi). Alternatively, and many animals, literally.

---

[23] Errico, Rocco A., and George M. Lamsa. *Aramaic Light on Ezekiel, Daniel, and the Minor Prophets: A Commentary Based on the Aramaic Language and Ancient Near Eastern Customs.* p. 165.
[24] IBID. p 165.

Certainly they are innocent and deserving of compassion, especially since they are many (Radak)."[25]

Thoughts

Jonah's anger with what happened in Nineveh is directed toward himself as a prophet because he knew that Israel would not listen to him yet an enemy of Israel did. It must have been frustrating to think that the people of the LORD would not accept the salvation the LORD offered but the foreigners did. Eventually the Assyrians destroyed the Northern Kingdom after they were warned by numerous prophets.

The other area to consider is monotheism. It

---

[25] Scherman, Nosson, and Meir Zlotowitz. "Chapter 3. Jonah" In *Jonah: The Later Prophets with a Commentary Antholigized from the Rabbinic Writings*. Brooklyn, N.Y: Mesorah Publications, 2014. p. 237.

was the LORD who offered salvation to the people of Nineveh. Ancient people believed that their gods were their gods alone. The Hebrews would have had the same attitude. The LORD was the creator of Heaven and Earth but was not the God of all people. It is clear in the Jonah story that the LORD was the God of all people because of the salvation to Nineveh. The development of monotheism would have taken centuries to develop and for the people to accept. So, the book of Jonah serves several purposes. Monotheism is one, salvation for all people, and when God wants you for a task it is best to do it.

Works Cited

Bowker, John. 2005. "Isaac Abravanel." In *The Concise Oxford Dictionary of World Religions*. Oxford: England: Oxford University Press.

Errico, Rocco and George Lamsa. 2012. *Aramaic Light on Ezekiel, Daniel and the Minor Prophets. A commentary based on the Aramaic Near Eastern Customs. Smyna, Georgia: Noohra Foundation*

http://jewishencyclopedia.com – The Jewish Encyclopedia

Scherman, Nosson, Meir Zlotowitz, Sheah Brander, and Menachem Davis. 2014. *The Prophets: The Later Prophets with a Commentary Anthologized from the*

Rabbinical Writings. Brooklyn, NY: Mesorah Publications.

www.ingramcontent.com/pod-product-compliance
Lightning Source LLC
Chambersburg PA
CBHW031410150726
47989CB00002B/599